MAKING SENSE OF IT: STRATEGIC ALIGNMENT AND ORGANIZATIONAL CONTEXT

John C. Henderson
James B. Thomas
N. Venkatraman

Working Paper No. 3475-92BPS   October 1992

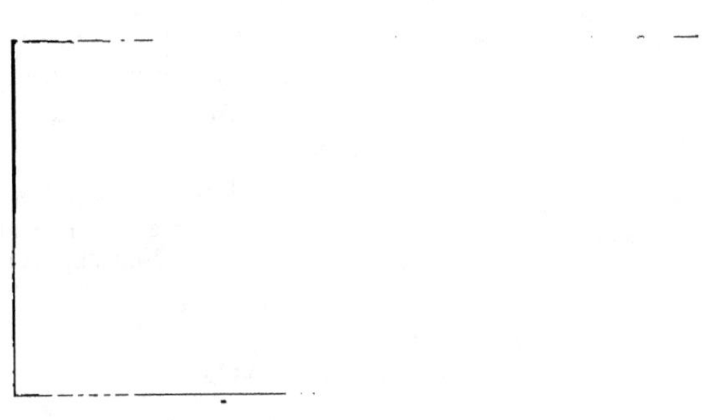

MAKING SENSE OF IT STRATEGIC ALIGNMENT AND
ORGANIZATIONAL CONTEXT

John C Henderson
James B Thomas
N Venkatraman

Working Paper No 3475-92BPS   October 1992

MAKING SENSE OF IT:
STRATEGIC ALIGNMENT AND ORGANIZATIONAL CONTEXT

John C. Henderson
Management Information Systems Department
School of Management
Boston University
704 Commonwealth Avenue
Boston, MA   02215
(617) 353-6142

James B. Thomas
Department of Management and Organization
Smeal College of Business Administration
Pennsylvania State University
University Park, PA   16802
(814) 865-2193

N Venkatraman
Sloan School of Management
E52-537
Massachusetts Institute of Technology
Cambridge, MA   02139
(617) 253-2660

An earlier version of this paper was presented at the Strategic Management
Society Conference in London, UK, October, 1992

MAKING SENSE OF IT:
STRATEGIC ALIGNMENT AND ORGANIZATIONAL CONTEXT

Abstract

This paper examines the relationship between top managers' understanding of the strategic alignment between the business and information technology (IT) domains and the organizational context in which that understanding is manifested Using responses from a nationwide survey of 393 top executives in the health care industry, we tested a series of hypotheses regarding the context-strategic alignment relationship We also examined the impact of two contingency variables· structure of the top management team and perceived environmental uncertainty Overall, the findings indicate systematic linkages between the information-processing activities (e.g , planning efforts) of top managers and their understanding of the critical relationships that define strategic alignment The specific relationships and contingencies found suggest that managers must manage the *context* in which they strive to make sense of their ambiguous environments as well as the *specific business and IT issues* they are forced to confront if they are to be successful in utilizing IT as a source of competitive advantage

INTRODUCTION

A widely-accepted assertion today is that information technology (IT) strategies and business strategies should be aligned (e g., Henderson and Venkatraman, 1992) for effective exploitation of IT capabilities and business transformations (Scott Morton, 1991) Within this general theme, research efforts have examined the linkage between business and IT planning (e g., King, 1978; Lederer and Mendelow, 1989), as well as the partnership between line and IT managers (e g , Henderson, 1990), as prescriptions for the required organizational transformations. Other have noted that the innovation reflected in the IT marketplace (e.g., communication capabilities and knowledge-based systems) have enabled firms to fundamentally change their market focus as well as their internal infrastructures (e.g., Keen, 1990). However, in spite of extensive writings pertaining to the need to align business and IT contexts, developing an IT-based strategic advantage remains a concept supported primarily by isolated anecdotes rather than the systematic, empirical investigation of appropriate antecedents (Boynton and Zmud, 1987, Venkatraman and Zaheer, 1990)

In this paper, we argue that attempts to create a *strategic* alignment between the business and IT domains of the firm are a function of the extent to which top managers understand the relationships between the critical components of *both* domains. This understanding is impacted by the organizational context that fosters (or impedes) the human information processing necessary to forge such an alignment More specifically, we contend that different organizational responses to the need to strategically align the firm's business and IT domains should be viewed from a managerial interpretation perspective (cf Daft and Weick, 1984) Such a perspective has served as a theoretical anchor for understanding why top managers respond differently to specific strategic events, developments or trends in the business environment (e.g., Milliken, 1990) as well as the IT environment (Ginsberg and Venkatraman, 1992). We subscribe to this theoretical anchor in this paper to empirically link top management's understanding of the relationship between business and IT domains to the organizational and environmental contexts in which that understanding is manifested.

Using responses from 393 top managers from a nationwide sample of 149 U S. hospitals, we tested a series of hypotheses underlying an operational model of *strategic alignment* We hypothesize that the internal organizational context (i.e., processes and structures that guide human information processing by top management team members) will be systematically related to the interpretation of the relationships that comprise strategic alignment. Further, we propose that the information processing capacity of the hospitals' top management team and the managers' perceived environmental uncertainty will moderate tne relationship between organizational context and the interpretations associated with strategic alignment

AN INTERPRETATION PERSPECTIVE

Organizations are composed of a broad set of concerns, structures, and processes that activate attention toward certain information (e.g , Dutton and Dukerich, 1991) and affect how top managers interpret or understand that information (e.g., Milliken, 1990). This organizational context constrains how issues are construed by making certain interpretations legitimate, by making different types of information available, and by motivating managers to frame the issues and information they confront in particular ways (Dutton, 1992)

A number of conceptualizations of this context/interpretation relationship have been discussed (e.g., Meyer, 1982, Kiesler and Sproull, 1982, Thomas and McDaniel, 1990). Daft and Weick (1984), Milliken (1990), and Ginsberg and Venkatraman (1992) propose that this relationship can be conceptualized as an ongoing sensemaking process composed of scanning, interpretation, and action This process entails the reciprocal interaction of information seeking, meaning ascription, and response (cf. Weick, 1979)

Scanning involves information acquisition for the purpose of finding (Pounds, 1969), recognizing (Cowan, 1986), or sensing (Kiesler and Sproull, 1982) strategic issues In the context of strategic IT development, organizational processes such as business and IT planning can be viewed as important mechanisms for searching the external environment (Hambrick, 1982) and the internal environment (Zmud, 1988) for problems, issues, or patterns (Dutton and Duncan, 1987). In this sense, they contribute to defining the internal organizational context that surrounds the sensemaking processes of top managers (Thomas and McDaniel, 1990).

Interpretation involves the development or application of ways of comprehending the meaning of information. It entails the fitting of information into some structure for understanding and action (Taylor and Crocker, 1981) The meaning ascription efforts linked to interpretation have received such labels as strategic issue diagnosis (Dutton, Fahey, and Narayanan, 1983), problem structuring (Abulsamh, Carlin, and McDaniel, 1990), and problem formulation (Lyles, 1981) Although these views differ in their breadth, each attempts to represent the process by which top managers in organizations translate events and develop an understanding of key concepts and relationships.

A basic premise of the interpretation perspective is that the way information is framed mobilizes action in a certain direction. For example, Dutton and Jackson (1987) note that the extent to which information is understood and interpreted can affect the level of risk taking, involvement, and commitment associated with strategic issues. Action also provides new data for subsequent scanning and interpretation efforts (cf. Milliken and Lant, 1991) which, in turn, facilitates learning and adaptation (Daft and Weick, 1984)

A growing body of research is beginning to provide insights into how managers' sensemaking efforts may be systematically influenced by contextual factors that dictate the information-processing efforts of top managers Examples of such studies include the impact of strategy on scanning and interpretation processes (Daft and Weick, 1984); how ideology impacts perceptions of, and reactions to, the environment (Meyer, 1982, Dutton and Dukerich, 1991); the relationship between the structure of the top management team and perceptions of a strategic issue (Thomas and McDaniel, 1990), and how uncertainty reduction mechanisms are linked to the interpretations of top managers (Milliken, 1990).

In this paper, we argue that the interpretation of key issues surrounding the competitive use of information technology is rooted in various scanning mechanisms that help comprise the internal information-processing context of the organization. More specifically, what determines a manager's inclination to persist or reorient the firm's use of IT is linked to how top managers perceive the nature of, and the relationships among, critical factors surrounding both the business and IT realms of the organization. These

perceptions are in turn systematically related to the information-gathering
mechanisms and constraints of the organization.

MAKING SENSE OF IT

Information technology has emerged as a critical component in the
strategies of many organizations (e g , Cash and Konsynski, 1985; Keen, 1990)
Indeed, over the last few years, the literature has offered numerous examples
and prescriptions that highlight the potential for IT to influence firm
strategies and market competencies (cf Scott Morton, 1991; Venkatrman and
Kambil, 1991).

Traditionally, the management of IT has been interpreted in terms of the
administrative and operational roles that IT play within the organization
(e.g., King, 1978). The *administrative* role defines the scope of IT as the
automation of specific functions such as payroll, accounts receivable, and
accounts payable. This role is reasonably well understood in the traditional
literature on management information systems (e g , Ein-Dor and Segev, 1978,
Ives, Hamilton, and Davis, 1980) and focuses on the deployment and management
of an efficient IT platform (i.e., hardware, software and communication
systems) for planning and control.

The *operations* role, which is an extension of the administrative role, is
distinguished by the creation and management of a technology platform that
creates the capability to automate the entire set of business processes as
opposed to only specific administrative activities. Unlike the administrative
role, this requires the management of an IT infrastructure that responds to
and supports the chosen business strategy of the organization (King, 1978,
McLean and Soden, 1981) Frameworks such as Business Systems Planning (IBM

5

Corporation, 1981) and Value Chain Analysis (Porter and Millar, 1985) reflect the logic underlying this role

A major trend in IT research and practice during the 1980's involved the use of IT to effect the competitive capability of the firm (e.g., McFarlan, 1984; Wiseman, 1985) This *competitive* role of IT required executives to extend their view of IT beyond an internal, efficiency focus to one that could enable new differential sources of competitive advantage in the marketplace (cf Keen, 1990, Rotemberg and Saloner, 1991) Indeed, many successful organizations can be distinguished by their ability to leverage IT capabilities to transform their competitive position (Scott Morton, 1991)

A wide range of conceptual frameworks have been proposed to help executives identify and assess the multitude of strategic issues that are inherent in this competitive role of IT. McFarlan (1984) and Wiseman (1985) emphasize the potential role of IT to effect *inter*-organizational processes and thus the ability to gain competitive advantage Others, such as Rockart and Scott Morton (1984) and Hammer and Mangurian (1987) emphasize the potential of IT to redesign the business processes in ways that result in fundamental *intra*-organizational changes that foster new competitive capabilities.

Throughout these efforts, there has been a constant demand to address the need to align business and IT strategies Walton (1989), for example, argues that alignment of strategies must go beyond the conventional notion of an IT plan that is linked to or responds to a business strategy. In a similar vein, Parker, Benson, and Trainor (1988) provide a framework for identifying strategic issues that address both the relationship between the IT and business domains, and issues inherent in the fit between a business strategy

6

and the design of the organization. These perspectives may be viable as frameworks for operationalizing the sensemaking processes of executives as they interpret IT strategic issues. However, as Henderson and Venkatraman (1992) noted, these frameworks provide two overarching dimensions upon which an operational model of alignment can be defined. *fit* (i.e., the alignment of the external and internal environments of the organization) and *linkage* (i e., the alignment of the business and IT domains of the firm). In this paper, we operationalize these dimensions of fit and linkage in terms of the strategic choices top executives must understand and in order to effectively implement the competitive role of IT

STRATEGIC ALIGNMENT

Concept of *Fit*

The concept of *fit* has emerged as an important concept in the organizational and strategy (e.g., Van de Ven and Drazin, 1985; Venkatraman, 1989) as well as the IT (e.g., Walton, 1989) literatures In simple terms, the proposition grounding this literature is that the "fit" (also termed integration, consistency, or contingency) between certain variables has significant positive implications for performance (cf. Venkatraman and Prescott, 1990) For example, fit in organizational research generally refers to the relationship between strategy and the external environment (e g , Jauch, Osborn, and Glueck, 1980). It also pertains to the internal designand processes necessary to execute this positioning such as structure (e g., Chandler, 1962; Rumelt, 1974) and administrative systems (Galbraith and Nathanson, 1978) This reflects the classic strategy formulation -- implementation alignment in the business domain, namely *business fit*.

However, as we consider the potential to leverage emerging IT
capabilities to redefine market structure characteristics (e.g , Clemons and
Row, 1988; Venkatraman and Kambil, 1991) as well as shape the basis for
competition (e g , Malone, Yates, and Benjamin, 1987), it becomes restrictive
to think of the "function" of information systems as subordinate to the
business domain of the organization. Indeed, just as the business domain of
the organization must be concerned with the external market, an emerging
recognition in the IT literature (e g , Scott Morton, 1991) is the importance
of an external *IT marketplace* consisting of new and emerging technologies
about which strategic interpretations and choices must be made to leverage the
functional-specific advantages of IT. As Henderson and Thomas (1992) suggest,
these strategic IT choices, and the competencies they imply, must then be
internally aligned with a supporting IT infrastructure. In this sense, we can
conceptualize the IT domain of the organization in a manner similar to the
business domain -- consisting of strategy formulation (i e , positioning the
firm in the IT marketplace) and strategy implementation (i e , design of a
supporting information systems infrastructure).

We can therefore specify a second type of fit, namely *IT Fit* Just as
the business strategy defines the organization's position in the external
business marketplace, an IT strategy defines the position of the organization
in the IT marketplace (Henderson and Venkatraman, 1992). Similarly, the IT
infrastructure is analogous to the organization's infrastructure in the sense
that it is defined as the internal arrangements of the IT domain (e.g ,
architectures, processes, etc.) To successfully execute the IT strategy it
is necessary to fit this external positioning with the internal arrangements
placed to manage the information systems function (Marcus and Robey, 1988)

Concept of *Linkage*

In its examination of the alignment between the business and IT domains, the IT literature has focused on two different types of relationships that we refer to as *functional linkage* and *strategic linkage*

Functional linkage refers to the relationship between organizational infrastructure and IT infrastructure. This link reflects the need to insure internal coherence between the organizational requirements on one hand, and the delivery capability of the information systems function on the other. For example, the design of the organization's infrastructure often determines the requirements for the IT infrastructure (e.g , Walton, 1989) Specifically, the design of key business processes (e g , just-in-time inventory systems) impacts the information products/services delivered by the IS function.

Strategic linkage refers to the relationship between business and IT strategies. That is, it is fundamentally concerned with the integration between the positions of an organization with respect to the business and IT marketplaces (Henderson and Sifonis, 1988) This linkage between these two strategies is a fundamental requirement for understanding the transformations required for realizing value from IT investments (McFarlan, 1984; Scott Morton, 1991). For example, the emergence of global information networks have both enabled and threatened the ability of multi-national firms to pursue wide-range global markets (Keen, 1986)

Thus, we can view the basic elements that must be interpreted and understood in any attempt to leverage IT as the fit and linkage between four areas business strategy, organizational infrastructure, IT strategy, and IT infrastructure. As Henderson and Venkatraman (1992) suggest, to maximize the probability of successfully utilizing IT as a competitive advantage, choices associated with each of these areas must be *strategically aligned* through fit and linkage.

Business Strategy

The concept of strategy is overarching (Andrews, 1980, Hax and Majluf, 1984) and covers a broad terrain with multiple meanings, definitions and conceptualizations (Venkatraman and Grant, 1986)   Throughout this work, however, at least three major factors are consistently identified as central to the operationalization of business strategy: (a) *business scope* - choices pertaining to product-market offerings (Hofer and Schendel, 1978, Porter, 1980); (b) *distinctive competencies* -- those attributes of strategy (e.g., pricing, quality, value-added service, superior distribution channels) that contribute to a distinctive, comparative advantage over other competitors (Snow & Hrebiniak, 1980; Prhalad and Hamel, 1990); and (c) *business governance* -- choices of interorganizational mechanisms to organize the business operations (e.g., strategic alliance, joint ventures, licensing arrangements) that recognizes the continuum between markets and hierarchy (Williamson, 1975)

Organizational Infrastructure

As with the concept of business strategy, the organizational literature has elaborated on the concept of organizational infrastructure. However, given the challenge to specify a parsimonious set of dimensions, we focus on three key factors: (a) *organizational design* -- including choices about organizational structure, roles and reporting relationships (Galbraith, 1977), (b) *processes* -- the articulation of workflows and the associated information flows for carrying out the key activities (Thompson, 1967); and (c) *skills* --

choices about the capabilities of organizational members needed to execute the
key tasks that support a business strategy (Fombrun, Tichy, and Devanna,
1984, Ulrich and Lake, 1990).

Information Technology Strategy

The concept of IT strategy is relatively new and hence open to differing
definitions and assumptions. Analogous to business strategy, we conceptualize
IT strategy as three key choices that position the firm in the IT marketplace:
(a) *information technology scope* -- refers to the types and range of IT
systems and capabilities (e.g., electronic imaging systems, local- and wide-
area networks, expert systems, robotics, etc) potentially available to the
organization in the IT marketplace (Keen, 1986), (b) *systemic competencies* --
focusing on those distinctive attributes of IT competencies (e.g., higher
system reliability, interconnectivity, flexibility) that contribute positively
to the creation of new business strategies or better support existing business
strategy (Scott Morton, 1991); and (c) *IT governance* -- choices of
interorganizational mechanisms (e.g., joint ventures, long-term contracts,
equity partnerships, joint R&D, etc.) to obtain the required IT capabilities,
involving issues such as the deployment of proprietary versus common networks
(Barrett and Konsynski, 1982, Rotemberg and Saloner, 1991) as well as
strategic choices pertaining to the development of partnerships to exploit IT
capabilities and services (Henderson, 1990; Johnston and Lawrence, 1988)

Information Technology Infrastructure

Analogous to organization infrastructure, this domain is defined in
terms of three dimensions· (a) *architecture* -- choices pertaining to
applications, data, and technology configurations (e g., Parker, Benson and

Trainor, 1988), (b) *processes* -- choices concerned with the work processes central to the operations of the IT infrastructure, including processes for systems development, maintenance, as well as monitoring and control systems (Henderson, Rockart, and Sifonis, 1987, Raghunathan and King, 1988); and (c) *skills* -- choices pertaining to the knowledge and capabilities required to effectively manage the IT infrastructure (Martin, 1982, Strassman, 1985).

The concepts of fit and linkage, and how they combine to define the extent of strategic alignment between the critical domains discussed above are presented in Figure 1. The model depicted in the figure constitutes a summary of the literature with respect to the primary set of choices that must be made if an organization is to successfully implement IT as a competitive advantage Collectively, this literature speaks to the importance of top managers being able to interpret how each element of the model (i.e., strategies and infrastructures) fit and link to become strategically aligned.

Insert Figure 1 about here

PROPOSITIONS AND HYPOTHESES

Understanding the factors that shape how top managers interpret the relationships in Figure 1 is critically important since it ultimately affects organizational actions and outcomes (Thomas, Clark, and Gioia, 1993; Dutton, Fahey, and Narayanan, 1983; Ginsberg and Venkatraman, 1992) Identifying the organizational characteristics that impact how top managers translate data into knowledge and understanding holds a prominent place in any attempt to understand the organizational change and learning required for utilizing IT as a source of competitive advantage (Venkatraman, 1991)

12

Even when exposed to identical markets or internal stimuli, top managers across, and within, organizations will come to different understandings of the relationships depicted in Figure 1 (e g , Boynton and Zmud, 1987) The understanding and the importance given to each of the relationships differ because prior theories, beliefs, cognitive structures, and organizational procedures influence the perceptions associated with each. Additionally, past actions are stored in a "retained set" (Hall, 1984 907) of organizational knowledge consisting of the memories of organization members, relationships, processes, and structures The resultant *organizational context* provides frameworks for deciding what will be attended to and how to understand the data that has been identified (Milliken and Lant, 1991).

Organizational Context

From an interpretive standpoint, organizational context can be viewed as those internal processes that impact how managers will interpret strategic events (Thomas and McDaniel, 1990). As delineated by Daft and Weick (1984), the critical aspect of these processes lies in their ability to facilitate the collection of data regarding actual and potential changes These search activities are seen as activators of strategic issue interpretation and subsequent action (e.g., Dutton and Duncan, 1987) and involve efforts to scan and assess the external environment (Hambrick, 1982) as well as the organization's internal environment (Cowan, 1986).

We chose three processes that embody the top manager's ability to gather information with respect to the elements of strategic alignment: (a) strategic planning efforts and (b) IT planning efforts (both of which represent the more formal aspect of information search in the strategic arena -- see McLean and

Soden, 1977, Venkatraman and Ramanujam, 1987); and (c) the partnership between
top management and the IT staff (which represents a more informal source of
information for top managers -- see Elam, 1988, Cooprider and Henderson,
1990). How each of these contextual factors relate to the understanding of,
and importance given to, the fit and linkage between the domains of strategic
alignment is hypothesized below. Phrased as a theoretical proposition, we
expect that:

> **Proposition** 1. *Scanning activities that comprise the internal
> organizational context will be systematically related to top managers
> understanding of strategic alignment*

Strategic Planning. Normative and descriptive writings have identified
the necessary capabilities of a strategic planning system (cf. Venkatraman and
Ramanujam, 1987) Traditionally, these include the planning system's ability
to anticipate surprises (Ansoff, 1975), its flexibility (Thompson, 1967), its
ability to facilitate control (Lorange and Vacil, 1977), and its role in
identifying opportunities (Taylor and Hussey, 1982) However, any measure of
an *effective* strategic planning effort must include the system's ability to
enhance the knowledge level of top managers (Hax and Majluf, 1991), the extent
to which planning identifies more relevant information (King and Cleland,
1978), and the planning systems ability to foster learning (Shrivastiva and
Grant, 1985)

As Ramanujam and Venkatraman (1987) found, the context of planning (i.e ,
the resources and effort applied to strategic planning by the organization)
has a dominant impact on planning effectiveness We therefore anticipate that
those organizations that have increased their efforts and commitment of
resources toward strategic planning in terms of time, involvement, education,

and implementation will be positively linked to how top managers interpret and
understand business fit.

> **Hypothesis 1a.** *Increased efforts in strategic planning will be related
> positively to top managers' understanding of business fit.*

Further, because one of the advantages to increased strategic planning efforts
is the generation of insights to the integration of diverse operations (Grant
and King, 1982), and to the enhancement of top managers' perceptions of
innovative opportunities at both the functional (Taylor and Hussey, 1982) and
strategic levels (Ginsberg and Venkatraman, 1992), we expect that.

> **Hypothesis 1b.** *Increased efforts in strategic planning will be related
> positively to top managers' understanding of strategic linkage*
>
> **Hypothesis 1c.** *Increased efforts in strategic planning will be related
> positively to top managers' understanding of functional linkage.*

IT Planning. IT planning is often classified as "strategic-IT planning"
and "systems planning " The focus of strategic IT planning is to integrate
the IS function with the other major functions of the organization while the
focus of systems planning is to ensure integration among subsystems and
hardware-software compatibility (Raghunathan and King, 1988; Boynton and Zmud,
1987). More specifically, IT strategic planning involves the assessment of
present and future technological environments as well as alternative IT
strategies (King and Srinivasan, 1983), while systems planning involves
assessing the coordination of IS with existing (or contemplated) projects,
programs, and processes (Henderson, Rockart, and Sifonis, 1987). Accordingly,
we expect that increased efforts in IT planning will lead to increased
understanding of IT fit and strategic linkage (i.e , the focus of the

traditional literature on IT strategic planning) and how the IT infrastructure
is linked to the infrastructure of the organization (i.e., functional linkage
-- the focus of IT systems planning)

> **Hypothesis 2a.** *Increased efforts in IT planning will be related
> positively to the top managers' understanding of IT fit.*

> **Hypothesis 2b.** *Increased efforts in IT planning will be related
> positively to the top managers' understanding of strategic linkage.*

> **Hypothesis 2c.** *Increased efforts in IT planning will be related
> positively to the top managers' understanding of functional linkage.*

IT Partnership   In the past, information systems (IS) and business
functions have each operated in separate worlds, with different languages and
only a minimal understanding of each other (Elam, 1988). A number of
researchers (e.g., Zmud, 1988; Cooprider and Henderson, 1990) suggest that a
partnership between the IS function and the rest of the organization -- a
relationship that is long term and involves the sharing of information,
benefits, and burdens -- is an important ingredient for organizational success
in light of the criticality of IT to market effectiveness and the increasing
complexity of building and operating the technology infrastructure.

One of the key ingredients in a strong partnership is the detailed
exchange of planning and operational information (Gardner and Cooper, 1988).
In this sense, each partner develops an appreciation and understanding for the
other's task environment (Lucas, 1984). Therefore, we anticipate that:

> **Hypothesis 3a.** *A strong partnership between top managers and IS
> management/staff will be positively related to top managers'
> understanding of IT fit.*

> **Hypothesis 3b.** *A strong partnership between top managers and IS
> management/staff will be positively related to top managers'
> understanding of strategic linkage*

Hypothesis 3c. *A strong partnership between top managers and IS management/staff will be positively related to top managers' understanding of functional linkage*

Moderators of the Context-Alignment Relationship

Information-processing structure of top management teams   Previous work has emphasized the importance of the structural aspects of context in terms of its impact on managerial interpretation of critical constructs (e g., Burgleman, 1983). Other work has provided more specific theoretical linkages For example, Thomas and McDaniel (1990) provide evidence that the information-processing capacity of the top management team provides a general environment that facilitates the chief executive officer's (CEO's) understanding of a strategic issue and the amount of information used during strategic decision processes. That is, the way a top management team is structured to process information limits or enhances the recognition of stimuli, the search for data, and the understanding of causal relationships.

Information processing characteristics such as high levels of participation and interaction among top managers and low levels of formalization facilitate more information processing (Galbraith, 1977) and foster extensive use of information (Daft and Lengel, 1986). Teams characterized by high information processing capacity impart a sense of mastery over critical decision variables since the executives feel they have surveyed, processed and understood the needed information (Eisenhardt, 1989). Without this capacity, planning and partnership efforts will not have the anticipated positive impact on managers' understanding of strategic alignment Thus, we propose that:

Proposition 2. *The pattern of relationships between organizational context and top managers' understanding of fit and linkage will be different for those managers in top management teams characterized by high versus low information-processing capacity.*

Perceived environmental uncertainty. Perceptions of information environments, especially perceptions of external environmental uncertainty, are important because they influence choices about the firm's strategy, structure, and processes (Huber and Daft, 1987, Miles and Snow, 1978) For example, Gordon and Narayanan (1984) found that perceptions of the environment affect decision processes including long-range planning (see also, Javidan, 1984). In a related study, Brown and Utterback (1985) found a positive relationship between perceived environmental uncertainty (PEU) and externally-directed communications activity suggesting that high PEU may lead to information-seeking activities directed toward the organization's external environment. These findings suggest that the PEU may distort or skew planning or partnership activities that provide input to the manager's interpretation of strategic alignment. Phrased as a theoretical proposition, our expectation is that:

Proposition 3. *The pattern of relationships between organizational context and top managers' understanding of fit and linkage will be different for those managers who perceive the environment as turbulent versus those who perceive it as more stable*

In summary, we expect that strategic and IT planning efforts, and the extent to which partnerships are developed between top management and the IT function, will be positively related to the understanding of strategic alignment. Further, this relationship will be moderated by the information processing capacity of the top management team and the managers' level of perceived environmental uncertainty. The propositions that define this model

of the relationship between context and strategic alignment are summarized in
Figure 2.

Insert Figure 2 about here

METHODS

Research Setting

We focused on a single industry to control for the impact of industry
characteristics on the perceptions of strategic alignment and chose the health
care industry for addressing the research questions of this study As Zajac
and Shortell (1989) note, in the 1980's health care organizations nation-wide
experienced an "environmental jolt" (Meyer, 1982) because of such events as
changes in regulation, clientele expectations, costs, and reimbursement
mechanisms. Amidst this turbulence, information technology has emerged as a
critical component in the business strategies of hospitals (Goldsmith, 1989)
Indeed, interest and investment in IT have grown at an accelerated pace in the
health care sector over the last five years leaving in its wake a gap between
the decision to invest in IT and the realization of benefits (Ball and Boyle,
1990). The gap highlights the criticality of understanding the elements of
strategic alignment if IT is to be successfully used in the health care sector
to initiate new strategies and transform business processes

Sample

A stratified sample of 161 hospitals was chosen to represent the
distribution of hospitals by region of the United States. All hospitals were
general-care facilities affiliated with two nation-wide health care systems

The hospitals in the first system (ALPHA) consisted of mostly urban/suburban facilities containing greater than 250 beds The second system (BETA) consisted mainly of smaller hospitals (<250 beds) in primarily rural areas Preliminary interviews with 27 top managers (both individually and in groups) from the respective corporate offices revealed that IT was perceived to be a critical driver of the strategies pursued by these hospitals.

Questionnaires were sent to members of the top management team (TMT) at each of the 161 hospitals with a cover letter from the appropriate system's chief executive officer urging participation in the study TMT membership for each hospital was established through input from corporate regional managers. Roles sampled included those of the administrator or chief executive officer, assistant administrator or chief operating officer, chief financial officer, director of medical affairs, and director of nursing; a small number of other administrative roles were also sampled (e.g , director of marketing).

Thus, we mailed questionnaires to 755 top-level administrators that represented an average of four administrators at each of the hospitals. A total of 481 questionnaires were returned (response rate=63.7%) representing 152 hospitals (response rate=94.4%). The number of respondents per hospital averaged 3.16 administrators and ranged from 1 to 5 top managers.

To assure that respondents were actively involved in the strategic management of the hospital, each was asked to indicate on a 1 (low) to 7 scale the extent to which they were involved in formulating and implementing the hospital's strategies and policies. Respondents who answered four or less to this question were eliminated from the analyses as being inappropriate for our research purposes. After these deletions, there were 393 usable questionnaire responses from 149 hospitals.

Respondents averaged 5.2 years in their respective roles and 5 6 years

spent in their hospital as a top manager Approximately 30% of the

respondents were hospital CEOs while 70% were other top managers (Chi-square

analysis revealed that in terms of position, respondents and non respondents

were not significantly different). The average size of the hospitals from

which we received responses was 199 beds. There was an approximate equal

split between the number of respondents from the two hospital systems

participating in the study Approximately 40% of the respondents

characterized their hospital as urban/suburban while 60% characterized their

hospital as rural. Corporate financial documents indicated that all hospitals

from which we received responses reported positive earnings for the quarter

prior to and during data collection.

Variables

The questionnaire included multiitem scales with 7-point Likert response

formats for all variables. The Appendix provides the complete scales for all

variables. Cronbach Alphas were greater than .70 for all scales (see Table

1); this meets the reliability criteria suggested by Nunnally (1978) The

specific data for each variable is presented in Table 1.

Fit and Linkage The two-way interrelationship between the four domains

(i.e., business strategy, IT strategy, organizational infrastructure, and IT

infrastructure) was measured in terms of the managers' understanding of, and

the importance given to, each.

Each measure of fit (i.e., business and IT) and linkage (i.e., strategic

and functional) consisted of a 6-item scale. Three items measured each of the

two, one-way interactions between the two domains that defined the fit or

linkage. For example, to ascertain the extend to which respondents understood
business fit, three items asked to what extent the respondent understood the
implications of strategic choices regarding *business strategy* on the
organization's infrastructure. Later, three items were posed to ascertain the
extent to which respondents understood the implications of choices regarding
organizational infrastructure on the business strategy of the hospital. The
six items were averaged to create a composite score of business fit. The same
procedure was used to calculate a score for IT fit, strategic linkage, and
functional linkage.

Strategic and IT Planning. Informants were asked to assess the extent to
which strategic and IT planning efforts in the hospital had changed over the
last three years. Specific dimensions included the extent to *time* spent on
the two planning efforts had increased, the degree to which top management
placed *importance* on the planning efforts, the extent of managerial
involvement in those efforts had increased, the extent to which planning
recommendations were *implemented* over the last three years, and the extent to
which efforts to *educate* managers regarding the role of these planning
processes had grown The five items from each of the planning scales were
averaged to calculate a strategic and IT planning score. Higher scores
indicated increased effort in planning over the last three years.

Partnership. The six-item partnership scale was based on Henderson
(1990) Partnership is defined as a coordinating strategy based on a long-
term relationship between senior management and the information systems
organization to achieve higher performance and/or lower costs through mutually
dependent action of independent actors. This relationship is measured along
two dimensions· (1) partnership in context (PIC), and (2) partnership in

action (PIA) (Henderson, 1990). PIC involves the longevity and stability of
the partnership. An example item was "To what extent does the information
systems staff and the top management of the hospital see their association as
a long-term relationship?" PIA is defined as the ability of members of the
partnership to influence the decisions that affect the partnerships
performance. An example item used to measure this dimension was "To what
extent do the members of the partnership have the ability to affect each
other's key decisions and policies?" Higher scores represented stronger
partnerships.

Information Processing Capacity. Information processing capacity refers
to the formality, interaction, and degree of participation among top managers
involved in executive decision processes at the hospital (Duncan, 1973). The
11-item scale used to measure information processing capacity was adapted from
Thomas and McDaniel (1990). The items were scaled so that higher scores
represented low formality, high participation, and high interaction indicating
an information processing structure with higher processing capacity. A sample
item was "To what extent is there a free and open exchange of ideas during
decision making?"

Perceived Environmental Uncertainty. The 10-item environment scale was
based on the dimensions of turbulence, complexity, and predictability (Downey
and Slocum, 1975; Huber and Daft, 1987) and made applicable to hospitals The
items were coded so that higher scores indicated a perceived turbulent,
complex and unpredictable environment within which the respondent's hospital
competed The following is a sample item "To what extent have the tastes and
preferences of patients in the marketplace changed?"

Control Variables

We controlled for relevant individual and organizational characteristics in the regression analyses. Four variables were chosen: role of the manager (1=CEO, 0=other), size of the hospital (number of licensed beds), location (1=urban/suburban, 0=rural), and system (1=ALPHA, 0=BETA).

Data Analysis

To test the hypothesized relationships between the dependent (i.e., business fit, IT fit, strategic linkage, and functional linkage) and the independent variables (i.e., strategic planning, IT planning, and partnership), we used multiple regression analyses. The four regression equations analyzed were:

$$\text{Business Fit} = a + b_1\text{control variables} + b_2\text{strategic planning} + b_3\text{IT planning} + b_4\text{partnership} + e \tag{1}$$

$$\text{IT Fit} = a + b_1\text{control variables} + b_2\text{strategic planning} + b_3\text{IT planning} + b_4\text{partnership} + e \tag{2}$$

$$\text{Strategic Linkage} = a + b_1\text{control variables} + b_2\text{strategic planning} + b_3\text{IT planning} + b_4\text{partnership} + e \tag{3}$$

$$\text{Functional Linkage} = a + b_1\text{control variables} + b_2\text{strategic planning} + b_3\text{IT planning} + b_4\text{partnership} + e \tag{4}$$

To examine the potential moderating effects of information processing capacity and perceived environmental uncertainty, the sample was divided using the median split of each   Equations 1-4 were then computed for each half and compared using the Chow test (see, Hambrick and Lei, 1985)

RESULTS

Table 1 presents means, standard deviations, Cronbach alphas for each scale, and Pearson zero-order correlations. Initial analysis using multivariate regression revealed that the set of dependent variables was related to the set of independent variables (Wilks s Lambda= 62, $F_{28,1346}$= 6.70, p< 001)

Insert Table 1 about here

Hypotheses

After controlling for role, size, system, and location, the regression analyses indicated that strategic planning was linked to the extent to which the top managers were knowledgeable of business fit (b=.23, p<.001). More specifically, top managers who perceived that their organizations had increased their strategic planning efforts over the last three years understood the nature and importance of the fit between business strategy and organizational structure more so than those managers who perceived their organizations had not increased their planning efforts Thus, Hypothesis 1a was supported (see Table 2)

The regression analyses also revealed that strategic planning efforts were significantly related to top managers' understanding of strategic linkage (b= 12, p<.05) However, while strategic planning facilitated understanding of the link between business and IT strategies (Hypothesis 1b), it did not have a significant effect on the level of understanding associated with the link between organizational and IT infrastructure Thus, Hypothesis 1c was not supported (see Table 2).

Insert Table 2 about here

We also found that IT planning was related to the level of knowledge and the importance afforded IT fit (b= 37, p<.001). Specifically, those top managers in hospitals that increased their efforts in IT planning over the last three years understood and perceived as important the concept of fit between IT strategy and the supporting IT infrastructure Thus, Hypothesis 2a was supported. IT planning was also significantly related to strategic linkage (b=.24, p< 001), as was predicted in Hypothesis 2b, and functional linkage (b=.30, p< 001), the focus of Hypothesis 2c (see Table 2). Thus, IT planning provided a mechanism for understanding both the strategic and functional relationships between the business and IT domains of the organization.

In terms of the impact of the partnership between line managers and IS management/staff on top managers' understanding of alignment, the regression analyses showed that partnership was significantly related to the IT fit (b= 15, p<.01), strategic linkage (b=.12, p<.05), and functional linkage (b=.18, p<.001) as predicted in Hypotheses 3a, 3b, and 3c, respectively (see Table 2). More specifically, the stronger the partnership, the more knowledgeable top managers were with respect to how business and IT strategies aligned with the supporting organizational and IT infrastructures of the organization.

A summary of the hypotheses-testing results is presented in Figure 3 in terms of an emergent model of how organizational context relates to the interpretation of strategic alignment.

Insert Figure 3 about here

Moderating Effects

A Chow test was applied to the regression results for each contingency(e.g , high vs. low information processing capacity) For IPC, the F-statistic calculated using the Chow test for each dependent variable showed that IPC was a significant contingency variable for predicting the level of understanding of business fit ($F_{(6,365)}$=24.83, p<.001), IT fit ($F_{(7,368)}$=2 78, p<.05), and functional linkage ($F_{(7,368)}$=2.33, p<.05). IPC did not contribute to the overall regression results when strategic linkage was the dependent variable. Thus, there was only partial support for Proposition 2. Chow test results also revealed that there was no overall difference in the regression equations for the high vs. low perceived environmental uncertainty conditions (all F <1 20). Thus, we did not find evidence to support Proposition 3

In terms of specific differences, we found that splitting the sample into high versus low IPC and high versus low PEU had little or no impact on the relationships between the planning variables (Strategic and IT) and top managers' understanding of alignment (see Tables 3 and 4). However, there were dramatic differences with respect to partnership. Specifically, while partnership played a significant role in understanding functional linkage (b=.23, p<.001) and IT fit (b=.17, p<.05) under conditions of low IPC, partnership was a significant factor in understanding only strategic linkage (b= 16, p<.001) under conditions of high IPC Similarly, while partnership was significantly linked to functional linkage (b=.33, p< 001) and IT Fit (b=.20, p<.001) when PEU was high, there was no partnership ties to the interpretation of alignment under conditions of low PEU By converting the corresponding betas to partial correlations and employing Fisher's Z-test (see

Hambrick and Lei, 1985), we found that the beta comparisons discussed above
were all significantly different at the p<.05 level.

Insert Tables 3 and 4 about here

Control Variables

The findings also indicate that the individual and organizational
characteristics used as control variables are linked to the interpretation of
strategic alignment. For example role (CEO vs. other) was found to be
negatively related to functional fit (beta=-.10, p<.05) but not related to any
of the other dependent variables. This suggests that managers below the top
level of management understand the link between business and IT
infrastructures more so than CEO's. This seems to be especially true for
managers in larger hospitals (beta=.10, p<.05). The control results also
suggest that the hospital system that the managers are in also facilitates or
impedes understanding of strategic alignment. Specifically, ALPHA managers
seemed to understand the business domain and its link to IT strategy much more
than managers from BETA (see Table 2) Interestingly, the system difference
continues irrespective of the level of information processing capacity (IPC) of
the top management team or the managers' perceptions of the hospital's
environmental uncertainty (PEU) (see Tables 3 and 4).

We also found that the role does not play a part in interpretations of
strategic alignment when IPC is high. Interestingly, managers in smaller
hospitals (not larger as found in the overall regression model) have enhanced
understanding of functional fit when IPC is high (beta=- 15, p<.05); but there
is no effect for size in low IPC environments

28

DISCUSSION

This study contributes to the current literature in three ways (1) it provides a theory-based framework (i.e., strategic alignment) that integrates the critical streams of research necessary for understanding the internally and externally related factors (as well as their relationships) surrounding the competitive use of IT; (2) it links the top managers' information-processing context to their understanding of the relationships that define strategic alignment; and (3) it provides initial insight to the contingencies that impact the context-alignment relationship.

Specific findings suggest that the three scanning variables play different roles in providing a context for understanding the concepts of fit and linkage -- the critical dimensions of *strategic alignment* For example, increased efforts in strategic planning were found to be the only contextual factor linked to the top managers' understanding of the "fit" between the business strategy and the infrastructure of the organization. What understanding top managers have of the fit between the organization's IT strategy and IT infrastructure seems to be acquired, at least in part, through the IT planning and partnership efforts of the organization These findings suggest that in terms of providing the informational "raw material" for interpreting critical issues associated with strategic alignment, IT and business functions continue to operate in separate worlds as observed by Zmud (1988).

Those top managers who felt they understood the linkage between the business and IT strategies of the organization appear to be from organizations that have increased their information processing capacity through increased

29

efforts in all three scanning activities -- strategic planning, IT planning, and partnership. As IT moves from its traditional administrative and operational role to a more competitive role in the organization (Rockart and Scott Morton, 1984), top management has been faced with the important challenge of developing, managing, and coordinating the cooperative relationships between the business and IT domains (Elam, 1988). Our results suggest that in order to understand the critical issues associated with such a trend, organizations must increase their human information processing efforts across all three fronts to expose managers to critical information

Not surprisingly, the results suggest that understanding the link between the business and IT infrastructures is enhanced by increased efforts in IT planning and partnership. This has been the traditional learning model for most organizations (Zmud, 1988). However, as Henderson and Venkatraman (1992) observe, decisions made that define the nature of this linkage, can impact subsequent change at the strategic level. More specifically, not fully understanding the implications of functional linkage decisions could limit or systematically bias the strategic choices made with respect to the other relationships that define strategic alignment. Therefore, as Henderson and Thomas (1992) suggest, strategic planning efforts must include recognition and discussion of these types of decisions to successfully utilize IT in its role of providing a competitive advantage

A number of interesting findings are revealed when we examine the moderating effects of perceived environmental uncertainty (PEU) and information processing capacity (IPC). While PEU was shown to not effect managers'*overall* understanding of strategic alignment, the manner in which specific factors impact understanding is altered under differing PEU

conditions. Specifically, strategic planning seems to impact the
understanding of strategic linkage issues only when managers perceive the
environment in which their hospital is positioned as more stable. This
suggests that coping with the complexity and intricacies of linking business
and IT strategies may be a luxury that can be afforded only when the
environment is perceived as stable enough to allow for more rational/
comprehensive analyses. Paradoxically, it may be under conditions of
turbulence that understanding the issues associated with strategic linkage is
most important.

Partnership appears to be related to understanding linkage and fit,
although the strength of this factor is moderated by both PEU and IPC. In
settings in which PEU is high, strong partnership between the IS and line
executives appears to significantly enhance both the executives' understanding
of IT fit and functional linkage. Taken together, IT and functional linkage
represent a *service* orientation embedded in the firm's planning processes
(Henderson and Thomas, 1992) That is, functional linkage reflects issues
concerning the definition and delivery of IT products/ services, while IT fit
reflects the issues involving the design and implementation of an IT strategy
and associated infrastructures. This suggests that when dynamism and
complexity are perceived as characterizing the market environment, line
managers utilize more informal relationships such as partnership as a means of
understanding the nature, and role, of effective IT products/services. In
more stable environments, the formal mechanisms of IT planning appear to have
the greatest impact on the executives understanding of the choices leading to
alignment

The specific effect of IPC on partnership's role in understanding strategic alignment is also interesting. For a context characterized by high levels of interaction and participation among top managers, a strong partnership appears to enhance understanding of strategic linkage This would suggest that the mechanisms by which IS executives can influence senior executive choices relating to business and IT strategies centers on informal processes that involve high participation rather than the more formal, analytical IT-planning processes often associated with IT-strategy formulation

Overall, the findings suggest an important link between the information-processing activities (e.g., planning efforts) of top managers and their understanding of the critical relationships (i.e., fit and linkage) that have their roots in both the strategy and IT literatures. The specific relationships and contingencies found in this study suggest that managers must manage the context in which they strive to make sense of their ambiguous environments and the specific business and IT issues they confront.

The strategic alignment model developed here represents a departure from the managerial interpretation literature in that the model captures the specific dimensions of an issue as opposed to the more general "analytical dimensions" (e.g., opportunity, threat, crises, etc.) that dominate that literature (Dutton, Stumpf, and Wagner, 1990) As Milliken (1990) and Lyles and Schwenk (1992) suggest, future work needs to examine the relationship between top managers' understanding of these frameworks and subsequent action and performance. This seems particularly appropriate for the more general issue of strategic alignment that is composed of the critical decisions that define most organizations (i e., strategy, structure, technology) Longitudinal work that would detect patterns and critical contingencies in the context-alignment relationship over time would also add to our understanding.

32

SUMMARY AND CONCLUSION

The IT literature is inundated with frameworks on how IT serves as a
source of strategic advantage. Many of these are normative in terms of how IT
could alter the basis for competition (e.g , McFarlan, 1984) or descriptive
checklists (e.g , Wiseman, 1985) which have a limited role in systematic
theorizing in this area. Specifically, we noted that there was a glaring
lack of attempts to delineate the process by which an organization *senses* the
potential role of IT, *interprets* its possible implications within a given
organizational context, as well as *acts* appropriately by allocating its
resources in order to derive significant benefits. This paper contributed to
the IT literature by providing a descriptive conceptual model of IT s role in
strategic management as well as applying the model through a managerial
interpretation framework to test a series of hypotheses. Thus, the
distinguishing characteristic of this paper lies not only in the conceptual
model, but also in our use of the model as the basis to introduce the
managerial interpretation perspective to IT research. We hope that this paper
will stimulate interested researchers to adopt the interpretation perspective
in other areas of IT research such as the adoption of IT innovations,
explanations of IT resource allocations including IT investments, and the
organization of the IT function

REFERENCES

Abulsamh, R., B. Carlin, and R. R. McDaniel, "Problem Structuring Heuristics in Strategic Decision Making," _Organizational Behavior and Human Decision Processes_, 45 (1990), 159-174.

Andrews, K. R., _The Concept of Corporate Strategy_, R. D. Irwin, Homewood, IL, 1980.

Ansoff, H. I., "Managing Strategic Surprise by Response to Weak Signals," _California Management Review_, 18 (1975), 21-33.

Ball, M. and T. M. Boyle, "Hospital Information Systems: Past, Present, and Future," _Hospital Financial Management_, 10 (1990), 12-24.

Barrett, S. and B. Konsynski, "Interorganization Information Sharing Systems, _MIS Quarterly_, Special Issue (1982), 93-105.

Boynton, A.C. and R.W. Zmud, "Information Technology Planning in the 90's: Directions for Practice and Research, _Management Information Systems Quarterly_, March (1987), 59-71.

Brown, J. W. and J. M. Utterback, "Uncertainty and Technical Communication Patterns," _Management Science_, 31 (1985), 301-311.

Burgelman, R. A., "A Process Model of Internal Corporate Venturing in the Diversified Major Firm," _Administrative Science Quarterly_, 28 (1983), 223-244.

Cash, J. J. and B. Konsynski, "IS Redraws Competitive Boundaries," _Harvard Business Review_, 63 (1985), 134-142.

Chandler, A. D., _Strategy and Structure_, MIT Press, Cambridge, MA, 1962.

Clemons, E. K. and M. Row, "McKesson Drug Company: A Case Study of Economost -- A Strategic Information System," _Journal of Management Information Systems_, 5 (1988).

Cooprider, J. G. and J. C. Henderson, "Partnership Between Line and IS Managers: A Management Model," _Working Paper 90-71_, Boston University, 1990.

Cowan, D. A., "Developing a Process Model of Problem Recognition," _Academy of Management Review_, 11 (1986), 763-776.

Daft, R. L. and R. H. Lengel, "Organization Information Requirements, Mediq Richness, and Structural Design," _Management Science_, 32 (1986), 554-571.

Daft, R. L. and K. E. Weick, "Toward a Model of Organizations as Interpretive Systems," _Academy of Management Review_, 9 (1984), 284-295.

Downey, H. K. and J. W. Slocum, Jr., "Uncertainty: Measures, Research and Sources of Variation," _Academy of Management Journal_, 18 (1975), 562-578.

Duncan, R., "Multiple Decision Making Structures in Adapting to Environmental Uncertainty: The Impact of Organizational Effectiveness," _Human Relations_, 26 (1973), 705-725.

Dutton, J. E., "The Making of Organizational Opportunities: An Interpretive Pathway to Organizational Change," In B. M. Staw and L. L. Cummings (Eds.), _Research in Organizational Behavior_, Greenwich, JAI Press, 1992.

Dutton, J. E. and J. M. Dukerich, "Keeping an Eye on the Mirror: Image and Identity in Organizational Adaptation," _Academy of Management Journal_, 34 (1990), 517-554.

Dutton, J. E. and R. B. Duncan, "The Creation of Momentum for Change through the Process of Strategic Issue Diagnosis," _Strategic Management Journal_, 8 (1987), 279-295.

Dutton, J. E., L. Fahey, and U. K. Narayanan, "Toward Understanding Issue Diagnosis," _Strategic Management Journal_, 12 (1983), 307-323.

Dutton, J. E. and S. E. Jackson, "Categorizing Strategic Issues: Links to Organizational Actions," _Academy of Management Review_, 12 (1987), 76-90.

Dutton, J.E., Stumpf, S.A., and D. Wagner, "Diagnosing Strategic Issues and Managerial Investment of Resources," in _Advances in Strategic Management_, JAI Press, (1990), 143-167.

Eisenhardt, K. M., "Making Fast Decisions in High-Velocity Environments," _Academy of Management Journal_, 32 (1989), 543-576.

Ein-dor, P. and E. Segev, "Strategic Planning for Management Information Systems," _Management Science_, 24 (1978), 1631-1641.

Elam, J. J., "Establishing Cooperative External Relationships," In J. J. Elam, M. J. Ginsberg, P. G. W. Keen and R. W. Zmud (Eds.), _Transforming the IS Organization_, ICIT Press, Washington, D.C., 1988.

Fombrun, C. J., N. M. Tichy, and M. A. DeVanna, _Strategic Human Resource Management_, Wiley, NY, 1984.

Galbraith, J. R., _Organization Design_, Addison-Wesley, Reading, MA, 1977.

Galbraith, J. R. and D. Nathanson, _Strategy Implementation: The Role of Structure and Process_, West Publishing, St. Paul, MN, 1978.

Gardner, J. and M. C. Cooper, "Elements of Strategic Partnership," In J. E. McKeen (Ed.), <u>Partnership: A Natural Evolution in Logistics</u>, Ohio State University, Cleveland, OH, 1988.

Ginsberg A. and N. Venkatraman, "Investing in New Information Technology: The Role of Competitive Posture and Issue Diagnosis," <u>Strategic Management Journal</u>, Summer (1992), 37-54.

Goldsmith, J., "A Radical Prescription for Hospitals," <u>Harvard Business Review</u>, 67 (1989), 104-111.

Gordon, L. A. and V. K. Narayanan, "Management Accounting Systems, Perceived Environmental Uncertainty and Organizational Structure: An Empirical Investigation," <u>Accounting, Organizations, and Society</u>, 9 (1984), 33-47.

Grant, J. H. and W. R. King, <u>The Logic of Strategic Planning</u>, Little, Brown and Company, Boston, 1982.

Hall, R. I., "The Natural Logic of Management Policy Making: Its Implications for the Survival of an Organization," <u>Management Science</u>, 30 (1984), 905-927.

Hambrick, D. C., "Environmental Scanning and Organizational Strategy," <u>Strategic Management Journal</u>, 3 (1982), 159-174.

Hambrick, D.C. and D. Lei, "Toward an Empirical Prioritization of Contingency Variables for Business Strategy," <u>Academy of Management Journal</u>, 28 (1985), 763-788.

Hammer, M., and G. E. Mangurian, "The Changing Value of Communications Technology," <u>Sloan Management Review</u>, Winter (1987), 65-71.

Hax, A. C. and N. S. Majluf, <u>Strategic Management: An Integrated Perspective</u>, Prentice-Hall, Englewood Cliffs, NJ, 1991.

Henderson, J. C., "Plugging into Strategic Partnerships: The Critical IS Connection," <u>Sloan Management Review</u>, 31 (1990), 7-18.

Henderson, J. C., J. F. Rockart, and J. G. Sifonis, "Integrating Management Support Systems into Strategic Information Systems Planning," <u>Journal of Management Information Systems</u>, 4 (1987), 5-23.

Henderson, J. C. and J. G. Sifonis, "The Value of Strategic IS Planning: Understanding Consistency, Validity, and IS Markets," <u>MIS Quarterly</u>, 12 (1988), 187-200.

Henderson, J. C. and J. B. Thomas, "Aligning Business and Information Technology Domains: Strategic Planning in Hospitals," <u>Hospital and Health Services Administration</u>, 37 (1992), 71-87.

Henderson, J. C and N. Venkatraman, "Strategic Alignment: A Model for
     Organizational Transformation throughInformation Technology Management,"
     in T. Kochan and M. Useem (Eds.), _Transforming Organizations_, Oxford
     University Press, (1992), 97-117.

Hofer, C. W. and D. E. Schendel, _Strategy Formulation: Analytical Concepts_,
     West Publishing, St. Paul, MN, 1978.

Huber, G. P. and R. L. Daft, "The Information Environments in
     Organizations," In F. M. Jablin, L. L. Putnam, K. H. Roberts, and L. W.
     Porter (Eds.), _Handbook of Organizational Communication_, Sage, Newbury
     Park, 1987.

IBM, "Information Systems Planning Guide," IBM Corporation, 1981.

Ives, B., S. Hamilton, and G. B. Davis, "A Framework for Research in Computer-
     based Management Information Systems," _Management Science_, 29 (1980),
     910-934.

Jauch, L. R., R. W. Osborn, and W. F. Glueck, "Short-term Financial Success
     in Large Business Organizations: The Environment-Strategy Connection,"
     Strategic Management Journal, 1 (1980), 49-63.

Javidan, M., "The Impact of Environmental Uncertainty on Long-Range Planning
     Practices of U.S. Savings and Loan Industry," _Strategic Management
     Journal_, 5 (1984), 381-392.

Johnson, H. R. and P. Lawrence, "Beyond Vertical Integration - The Rise of
     Value-adding Partnerships," _Harvard Business Review_, 66 (1988), 94-101.

Keen, P. G. W., _Competing in Time: Using Telecommunications for Competitive
     Advantage_, Ballinger, Cambridge, MA, 1986.

Keen, P. G. W., "Telecommunications and Organizational Choice," in Fulk and
     Steinfield (Eds.), _Communication Technology_, Sage, New York, 1990.

Kiesler, S. and L. Sproull, "Managerial Response to Changing Environments:
     Perspectives on Problem Sensing from Social Cognition," _Administrative
     Science Quarterly_, 27 (1982), 548-570.

King, W. R., "Strategic Planning for Management Information Systems," _MIS
     Quarterly_, 2 (1978), 27-37.

King, W. R. and D. I. Cleland, _Strategic Planning and Policy_, Van Nostrand
     Reinhold, NY, 1978.

King, W. R. and A. Srinivasan, "Decision Support Systems: Planning,
     Development, and Implementation," _Applications in Management Science_, 3
     (1983), 87-107.

Lederer, A. L. and A. L. Mendelow, "Coordination of Information Systems Plans
     with Business Plans," _Journal of Management Information Systems_, Fall
     (1989), 5-19.

Lorange, P. and R. F. Vancil, _Strategic Planning Systems_, Prentice-hall,
     Englewood Cliffs, NJ, 1977.

Lucas, H. C., "Organization Power and the Information Services Department,"
     Communications of the ACM, 27 (1984), 58-65.

Lyles, M. A., "Formulating Strategic Problems: Empirical Analysis and Model
     Development," _Strategic Management Journal_, 2 (1981), 61-75.

Lyles, M. A. and C. R. Schwenk, "Top Management, Strategy, and Organizational
     Knowledge Structures," _Journal of Management Studies_, 29 (1992), 155-174.

Malone, T. W., J. Yates, and R. I. Benjamin, "Electronic Markets and
     Electronic Hierarchies," _Communications of the ACM_, (1987), 484-497.

Marcus, M. L. and D. Robey, "Information Technology and Organization Change:
     Causal Structure in Theory and Research," _Management Science_, 34
     (1988), 583-598.

Martin, J., _Application Development Without Programmers_, Prentice-hall,
     Englewood Cliffs, NJ, 1982.

Mason, R. O., "Dialectical Approach to Strategic Planning," _Management
     Science_, 15 (1969), 403-414.

McFarlan, F. W., "Information Technology Changes the Way You Compete,"
     Harvard Business Review, 62 (1984), 98-108.

McLean, E. R. and J. V. Soden, _Strategic Planning for MIS_, John Wiley, New
     York, 1977.

Meyer, A. D. "Adapting to Environmental Jolts," _Administrative Science
     Quarterly_, 27 (1982), 515-536.

Miles, R. E. and C. C. Snow, _Organizational Strategy, Structure, and
     Process_, McGraw-Hill, NY, 1978.

Milliken, F. J., "Perceiving and Integrating Environmental Change: An
     Examination of College Administrators' Interpretation of Changing
     Demographics," _Academy of Management Journal_, 33 (1990), 42-63.

Milliken, F. J. and T. K. Lant, "The Effect of an Organization's Recent
     Performance History on Strategic Persistence and Change," in _Advances in
     Strategic Management, Volume 7_, (1991), 129-156.

Parker, M. M., R. J. Benson, and H. E. Trainor, _Information Economics: Linking Business Performance to Information Technology_, Prentice-Hall, Englewood Cliffs, NJ, 1988.

Porter, M. S., _Competitive Strategy_, The Free Press, New York, 1980.

Porter, M. E., and V. E. Millar, "How Information Gives You Competitive Advantage," _Harvard Business Review_, July-August (1985), 149-160.

Pounds, W. F., "The Process of Problem Finding," _Industrial Management Review_, 11 (1969), 1-19.

Prahalad, C. K. and G. Hamel, "The Core Competence of the Corporation," _Harvard Business Review_, May (1990), 79-92.

Raghunathan, T. S. and W. R. King, "The Impact of Information Systems Planning on the Organization," _Omega_, 16 (1988), 85-93.

Ramanujam, V. and N. Venkatraman, "Planning Systems Characteristics and Planning Effectiveness," _Strategic Management Journal_, 8 (1987) 453-468.

Rockart, J. F. and M. S. Scott Morton, "Implications of Changes in Information Technology for Corporate Strategies," _Interfaces_, 14 (1984), 84-95.

Rotemberg, J. and G. Saloner, "Information Technology and Strategic Advantage," In M. S. Scott Morton (Ed.), _The Corporation of the 90's_, Oxford University Press, 1991.

Rumelt, R., _Strategy, Structure and Economic Performance_, Harvard University Press, Cambridge, MA, 1974.

Scott Morton, M., _The Corporation of the 90's: Information Technology and Organizational Transformation_, Oxford University Press, New York, 1991.

Shrivastiva, P. and J. H. Grant, " Empirically Desired Models of Strategies Decision-Making Process," _Strategic Management Journal_, 6(1985), 97-113.

Snow, C. C. and L. Hrebiniak, "Strategy Distinctive Competence and Organizational Performance," _Administrative Science Quarterly_, 25 (1980), 317-336.

Strassman, P., _The Information Payoff_, Free Press, NY, 1985.

Taylor, B. and D. Hussey, _The Realities of Planning_, Pergamon Press, NY, 1982.

Taylor, S. E. and J. Crocker, "Schematic Bases for Social Information Processing," In E. T. Higgins, C. P. Herman, and M. P. Zanna (Eds.), _Social Cognition_, LEA, Hillsdale, 1981, 89-133.

Thomas, J. B., S. M. Clark, and D. A. Gioia, "Strategic Sensemaking and Organizational Performance: Linkages among Scanning, Interpretation, Action, and Outcomes," _Academy of Management Journal_, forthcoming, 1992.

Thomas, J. B. and R. R. McDaniel, "Interpreting Strategic Issues: Effects of Strategy and Information Processing Structure of Top Management Teams," _Academy of Management Journal_, 33 (1990), 286-306.

Thompson, J. D., _Organizations in Action_, McGraw-Hill, NY, 1967.

Ulrich, D and D. Lake, _Organizational Capability: Competing from the Outside Out_, New York: Wiley, 1990.

Van de Ven, A. and R. Drazin, "The Concept of Fit in Contingency Theory," In L. L. Cummings and B. W. Staw (Eds.), _Research in Organizational Behavior, Volume, 7_, JAI Press, NY, 1985, 333-365.

Venkatraman, N., "The Concept of Fit in Strategic Research: Toward Vebal and Statistical Correspondence," _Academy of Management Review_, 14 (1989), 423-444.

Venkatraman, N., "Information Technology-Induced Business Reconfiguration: The New Strategic Management Challenge," In M. S. Scott Morton (Ed.), _The Corporation of the 90's_, Oxford University Press, 1991.

Venkatraman, N. and J. H. Grant, "Construct Measurement in Organizational Strategy Research: A Critique and Proposal," _Academy of Management Review_, 11 (1986), 71-87.

Venkatraman, N. and A. Kambil, "The Check's Not in the Mail: Strategies for Electronic Integration in Tax-return Filing," _Sloan Management Review_, 31 (1991).

Venkatraman, N. and J. E. Prescott, "Environment-Strategy Coalignment: An Empirical Test of Its Performance Ramifications," _Strategic Management Journal_, 11 (1990) 1-23.

Venkatraman, N. and V. Ramanujam, "Planning System Success: A Conceptualization and an Operational Model," _Management Science_, 33 (1987), 687-705.

Venkatraman, N. and A. Zaheer, "Electronic Integration and Strategic Advantage: A Quasi-Experimental Study in the Insurance Industry," _Information Systems Research_, 1 (1990).

Walton, R. E., _Up and Running: Integrating Information Technology and the Organization_, Harvard Press, Boston, 1989.

Weick, K. E., _The Social Psychology of Organizing_, Addison-Wesley, Reading, MA, 1979.

Williamson, O. E., _Markets and Hierarchies_, Free Press, NY, 1975.

Wiseman, C., _Strategy and Computers: Information Systems as Competitive Weapons_, Dow Jones-Irwin, Homewood, IL, 1985.

Zajac, E. J. and S. M. Shortell, "Changing Generic Strategies: Likelihood, Direction, and Performance Implementations," _Strategic Management Journal_, 10 (1989), 413-430.

Zmud, R. W., "Building Relationships Throughout the Corporate Family," In J. J. Elam, M. J. Ginsberg, P. G. W. Keen, and R. W. Zmud (Eds.), _Transforming the IS Organization_, ICIT Press, Washington, DC, 1988, 55-83.

Items from Questionnaire Scales

Dependent Variables

All relevant terms were defined prior to posing questions regarding
specific relationships. Pictorial representations of the relationships were
also provided for each fit and linkage variable. Responses for each scale
ranged from 1 (to a small extent) to 7 (to a great extent).

Business Fit

Indicate the extent to which the executive team is knowledgeable and
understands the implications of business strategy choices on decisions
concerning. .

1...organizational structure, reporting relationships, roles, etc
2   business processes, work flows, etc.
3.. human resources for line or functional areas

Indicate the extent to which the executive team is knowledgeable and
understands the implications of organizational structures and processes on
decisions concerning ..

4.. product/service and market scope such as range, segment, etc.
5...distinctive business characteristics such as quality, price, or service.
6.. strategic alliances with customers, suppliers or intermediaries.

IT fit

Indicate the extent to which the executive team is knowledgeable and
understands the implications of choices concerning IT infrastructure and
processes on decisions concerning...

1. information technology scope such as telecommunications, expert systems,
    etc
2. distinctive IT system characteristics such as reliability, connectivity,
    costs, etc.
3. IT focused alliances or partnerships such as joint ownership of
    telecommunications, jointly developed software, etc.

Indicate the extent to which the executive team is knowledgeable and
understands the implications of choices concerning IT strategy on decisions
concerning...

4...IT infrastructure such as applications, databases or hardware
5   IT processes and operations such as the systems development process, data
    center operations, etc.
6   .IT human resources, skills, values, etc

Strategic Linkage

Indicate the extent to which the executive team is knowledgeable and
understands the implications of IT strategy choices on decisions concerning...

1 ..business scope, e.g., key products/services, markets, etc.
2 ..business characteristics such as quality, price, service level, etc.
3...strategic alliances with customers, suppliers, or intermediaries.

Indicate the extent to which the executive team is knowledgeable and
understands the implications of business strategy choices on decisions
concerning

4 ..information technology scope such as image processing, telecommunications,
   etc.
5 ..distinctive IT system characteristics such as reliability, connectivity,
   costs, etc.
6...IT-focused alliances or partnerships such as joint ownership of
   telecommunications, jointly developed software, etc

Functional Linkage

Indicate the extent to which the executive team is knowledgeable and
understands the implications of choices concerning organizational structure
and process on decisions concerning ..

1 ..IT infrastructure such as key applications, databases, or hardware
2...IT processes and operations such as the systems development process, data
   center operations, etc.
3 ..IT human resources, skills and values, etc.

Indicate the extent to which the executive team is knowledgeable and
understands the implications of choices concerning IT infrastructure and
processes on decisions concerning...

4 ..organizational structure, reporting relationships, roles, etc.
5 ..hospital processes, work flows, etc
6...human resources for line or functional areas

Independent Variables

Strategic Planning (1=to a small extent, 7=to a great extent)

To what extent. .
1...has the time spent by management on strategic business planning changes
   over the last 3 years?
2.. have the actions and recommendations resulting from the strategic business
   planning process been implemented in the hospital?

43

3...has strategic business planning been viewed as an important aspect of top
   management?
4...has the time spent by top management in strategic business planning
   increased over the last 3 years?
5...has your hospital been investing in programs to educate top management
   about the strategic business planning?

IT Planning (1=to a small extent, 7=to a great extent)

To what extent...
1 . has the involvement of information systems managers in IT planning
   increased over the last 3 years?
2.. has the time spent by top management in IT planning increased over the
   last 3 years?
3...has your hospital been investing in programs to educate top management
   about the role of IT planning?
4...has the overall emphasis on the importance of IT planning increased over
   the last 3 years?
5.. have the actions and recommendations resulting from IT planning process
   been implemented in the hospital?

Partnership (1=very weak; 7=extremely strong).

1.   In general, the ability of our IT staff and top management to work
     together is
2.   In general, the level of influence that our IT staff and top management
     have on the other's key decisions and policies is:
3.   In general, the degree to which our IT staff and top management believe
     that the effective management of IT will generate long-term benefits for
     our hospital is:
4.   In general, the day-to-day working relationship between our IT staff and
     top management is:
5.   In general, the degree to which our IT staff and top management view
     their association as a long-term relationship is
6.   In general, the ability of members of the partnership to affect each
     other's key decisions and policies is:

Information Processing Capacity (1=to a small extent, 7=to a great extent)

To what extent...
1...do you feel that you have the opportunity to express your ideas?
2...do you feel other executives team members' ideas are imposed upon you?
3...are written rules and procedures followed?
4...do you feel your views are included in executive decisions?
5...do you interact with other team members on an informal basis?
6...do committees such as ad hoc task groups form?
7...do one or two people dominate the handling of the planning process?
8...is there a free and open exchange of ideas during decision making?

9   is the strategic decision process formal and/or rule-oriented?
10   is the strategic decision process participative?
11   do participants interact?

Perceived Environmental Uncertainty

1   The group of hospitals who are your key competitors in our marketplace
     during the last 3-5 years has (1=remained stable; 7=radically changed)
2   The tastes and preferences of your patients in our marketplace have:
     (1=become much less stable, 7= become much more stable)
3   The market activities of your key competitors have: (1=become far less
     predictable; 7=become far more predictable)
4.   The rate of innovation of new products and services offered by other
     health care institutions in your marketplace has: (1=fallen dramatically,
     7=increased dramatically)
5.   Please indicate the degree of competitive pressure on your hospital from
     new competitors in your marketplace: (1=none, 7=intense)
6   The size of our market has remained fairly constant over the past 3-5
     years: (1=disagree; 7=agree)
7.   During the next 3-5 years we expect to see significant competition from
     health care (or other) institutions that have not been our traditional
     competitors: (1=disagree; 7=agree)
8   The market activities of our competitors become: (1=far less hostile,
     7=far more hostile)
9   The market activities of our key competitors now affect the hospital in.
     (1=far fewer ways, 7=many more ways)
10   The needed diversity of our service methods and marketing tactics to cater
     to our patients has: (1=dramatically decreased; 7=dramatically increased)

TABLE 1

Means, Standard Deviations, Alphas and Zero-Order Correlations (N=393)

<u>Variables</u>

Alignment	Mean	S D	Cronbach Alpha	1	2	3	4	5	6	7
1 Business Fit	5 13	1 02	.91	--						
2 IT Fit	3 63	1.28	.96	.39***	--					
3. Strategic Linkage	4 45	1 09	.89	46***	.67***	--				
4 Functional Linkage	3.99	1.24	.94	50***	79***	.70***	--			
Context										
5 Strategic Planning	4.74	1 04	75	24***	19***	29***	.31***	--		
6. IT Planning	3 89	1 44	.88	16***	38***	.36***	.43***	.56***	--	
7 Partnership	4 45	1.17	92	27***	29***	.29***	.35***	.36***	50***	--
Moderators										
8 Environment	4 67	.74	71	.05***	- 11*	-.05	-.11*	.17***	-.01	-.07
9 Info Processing Structure	5 34	.97	85	.28***	02	.03	.10*	25***	13**	.20***

* p < .05
** p < .01
*** p < .001

TABLE 2

Multiple Regression Results[a]

	Alignment Variables			
Independent Variables	Strategic Linkage	Functional Linkage	Business Fit	IT Fit
Control				
Role	$-.09^t$ (.11)	$-.10^*$ (.12)	04 (.11)	$-.09^t$ (.13)
Size	$-.08$ (.00)	10^* (.00)	-03 (.00)	-06 (.00)
Location	$-.05$ (.12)	01 (.13)	-04 (.11)	00 (.14)
System	$.11^*$ (.12)	07 (.13)	$.24^{***}$ (.11)	.03 (.14)
Context				
Strategic Planning	12^* (.06)	$.07^{***}$ (.07)	23^{***} (.06)	$-.08^{***}$ (08)
IT Planning	24^{***} (05)	$.30^{***}$ (.06)	04 (.05)	$.37^{***}$ (06)
Partnership	12^* (05)	$.18^{***}$ (.06)	-----	$.15^{**}$ (.06)
df	7,376	7,376	6,377	7,376
F	11.37^{***}	$16\ 69^{***}$	$8\ 38^{***}$	11.49^{***}
R^2	17	24	.12	18

[a] Standardized beta reported with standard error in parentheses

t p < 10
$*$ p < 05
$**$ p < 01
$***$ p < 001

TABLE 3

Multiple Regression Results Using Perception of
Environment as Moderator[a]

Independent Variables	Perceived Stability				Perceived Turbulence			
	Strategic Linkage	Functional Linkage	Business Fit	IT Fit	Strategic Linkage	Functional Linkage	Business Fit	IT Fit
Control								
Role	- 06	- 07	.07	- 11^t	- 11	- 14*	02	- 07
Size	- 08	-.13^t	-.06	- 12^t	- 09	- 07	-.01	-.01
Location	-.08	-.05	- 05	-.10	- 03	10	-.06	10
System	15*	.14^t	.23***	06	07	02	25***	01
Context								
Strategic Planning	15*	07	- 27***	-.05	09	.09	.20*	- 11***
IT Planning	25**	38***	.07	.38***	23*	21*	01	35**
Partnership	09	03	--	.08	12	33***	--	.20**
df	7,184	7,184	6,185	7,184	7,184	7,184	6,185	7,184
F	7 19***	7.73***	5 61***	6 20***	4 36***	10 74***	3 34**	5.48***
R^2	20	21	14	.18	16	.32	11	.19

[a]Standardized beta is reported.

^{t}p < .10
*p < .05
**p < .01
***p < .001

TABLE 4

Multiple Regression Results Using Perception of
Information Processing Capacity (IPC) as Moderator[a]

	Perceived High IPC				Perceived Low IPC			
Independent Variables	Strategic Linkage	Functional Linkage	Business Fit	IT Fit	Strategic Linkage	Functional Linkage	Business Fit	IT Fit
Control								
Role	- 01	- 05	07	03	- 18**	- 20***	- 06	-23**
Size	- 10	-.15*	-.05	- 11	- 05	- 03	- 04	01
Location	- 07	04	-.14*	- 01	- 03	01	.05	02
System	18*	14^t	.30***	09	03	- 02	.16*	- 03
Context								
Strategic Planning	11	14	.23**	- 10	14^t	00	.16^t	- 05
IT Planning	20*	20*	- 01	31**	32***	43***	.16^t	46**
Partnership	16*	10	--	.13	08	23***	--	17*
df	7,184	7,184	6,185	7,184	7,184	7,184	6,185	7,184
F	4.76***	4 74***	5 89***	3.16**	8 33***	15 90***	3.41**	12.56*
R^2	.15	15	16	.11	24	38	.10	.32

[a]Standardized beta is reported

^{t}p < 10
*p < 05
**p < 01
***p < 001

Figure 1
Conceptual Model:
Fit, Linkage, and Domains of Strategic Alignment

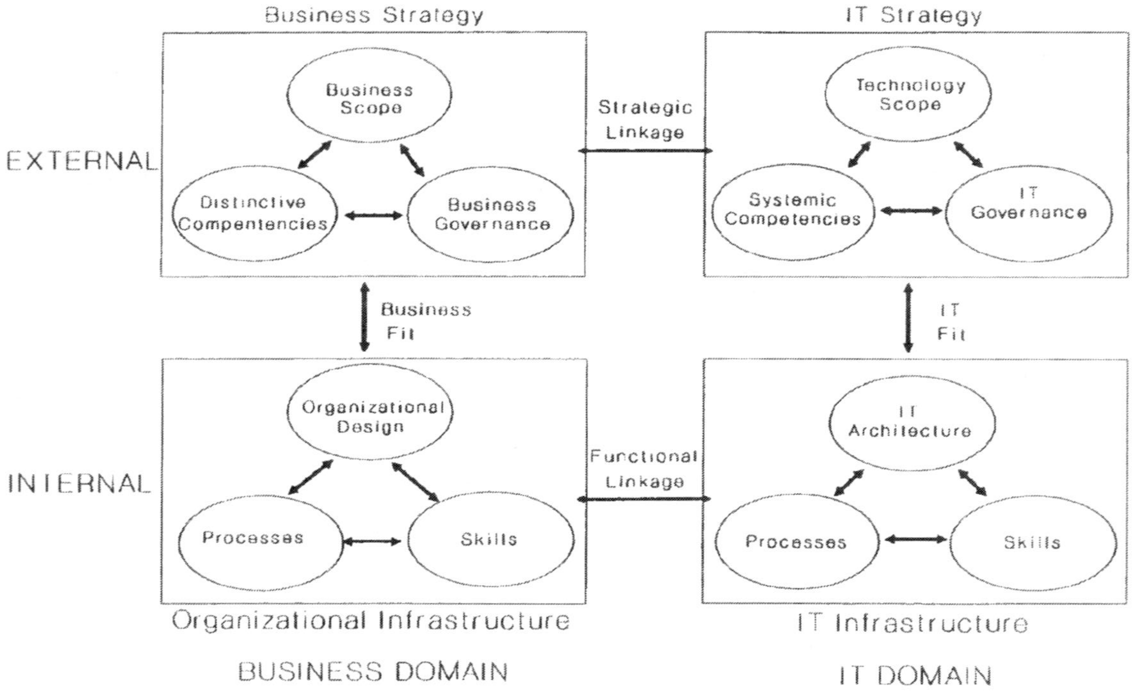

Figure 2
Model of the Relationship between
Context and Strategic Alignment

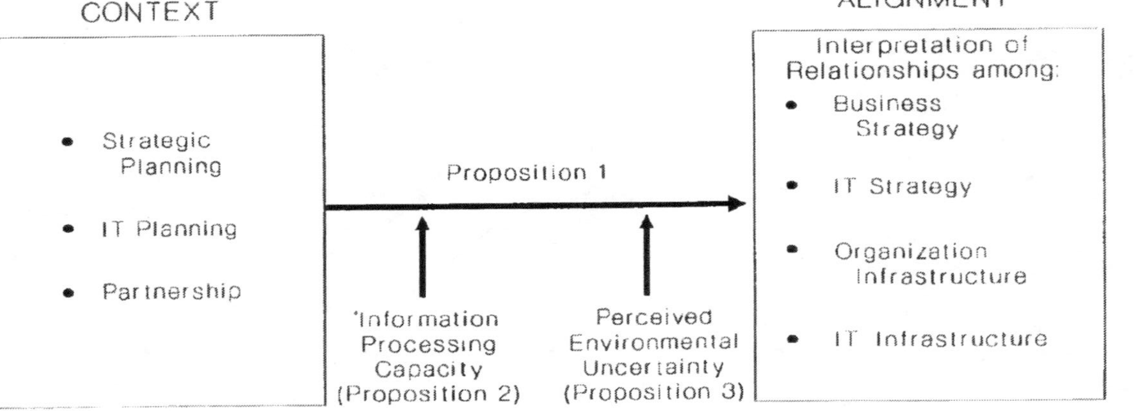

Figure 3
Summary of Results[a]

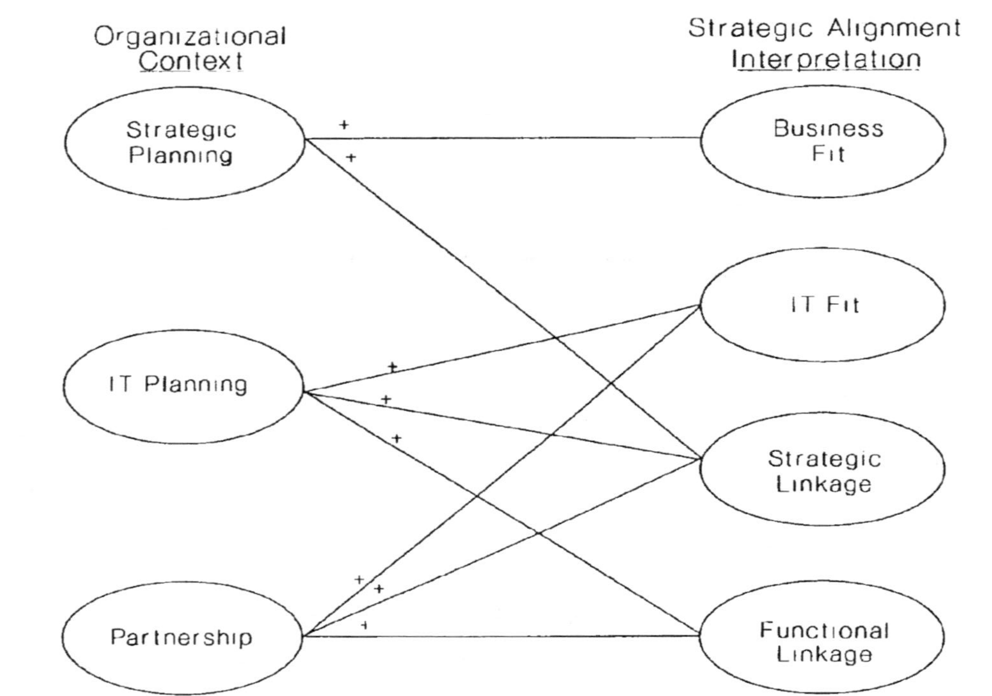

[a] For all relationships p< 05